You'll Thank Me Later

A Guide To Nurturing Gratitude In Our Children
(And why that matters)

By Annie M. Zirkel

This book is a big thank you to my mom and dad
It may have taken a while to show you the fruits of your labors
but I am eternally grateful for all you have taught me.

Acknowledgements in a book about gratitude could go on and on, but I'll try to be brief. Thanks to my excellent husband, Ed, for believing in me and having my back; my three awesome boys - Alex for his simple inspiration, Adam for his great feedback, and Nicky for his wise insights; my editor, James Borda for his wordsmithing and for being a kind pushy person; my energetic marketing team Jenna Cortis, Crystal McLain and Brian Bruman.

And to all my family and friends - you know who you are - that believed in the importance of this material, and me.

ISBN 978-0-615-32777-8

Az Is Publishing
P.O. Box 8276, Ann Arbor, MI, 47107-8276
www.azispublishing.com • 2009

Table of Content

Table of Contents

Table of Content

Introduction - Planting The Seed

Gratitude is not only the greatest of virtues, but the parent of all the others. ~ **Cicero, Roman philosopher, statesman**

One day, somewhere around 1910, a poorly dressed man entered a German deli in Ridgewood, NY begging for food. The teenager behind the counter ran to get the owner. When the owner came out from the back, the man explained that he was literally penniless, and had a wife and child who were starving. Could they please spare a bottle of milk and some bread?

Within minutes, the homeless family began a one-week stay as guests in my Great-Grandma Neumann's meager attic. It wasn't much, but it was warm and safe.

The teenager behind the counter was my grandmother, and this story was passed on by my father who holds this account in high regard. He writes:

I am so thankful for that spontaneous action, typical of the stories I heard. My grandparents worked hard - 14 hour a day - for little monetary reward but compared to many at the time they were well off. Sharing what they could was their way of expressing gratitude for their good fortunes.

I've told that story countless times, and rejoice when I see similar acts duplicated and triplicated among my nine children and twenty-five grandchildren. A genuine act of kindness is still cascading blessings on the lost and least and lonely, more than 90 years later.

My father's mother - my grandmother - grew up, got married and raised 8 children. My memories of her are a bit distant except that when we visited her in Queens, I was always drawn to her garage where she had a perpetual garage sale going on to raise money for the Medical Missions Sisters of India.

Eventually she moved in with my aunt and cousins. My cousin, Mary, recounted her experience with Grandma.

Grandma was always spouting sayings like..."I felt sorry for myself that I didn't have a new coat, till I met a woman who had no coat", or "I felt bad that I didn't get a seat on the bus, until I saw a neighbor walking home due to lack of bus fare". She was constantly trying to point out that what we had was enough to be grateful for and that in reality, we had more than enough, and we needed to share it with those who did not. It's how to keep life in perspective, to be grateful for all the wonderful things in our lives that didn't have material or monetary value - a good friend, a kind gesture, a beautiful sunset, a great memory.

At the time, I thought she was a little over the top, and she was, but as it turned out - that was a good thing.

There are other stories about both my father's parents and the messages of gratitude that they instilled in my dad.

My mother too came from such a family, with charity and hospitality a central theme, even though they had little to share and 9 mouths to feed. Meager beginnings meant gratitude for the smaller things. An extra trinket in a Christmas stocking, a good sing-a-long around the piano. And though at 17, my mom was forced to fill her mother's prematurely empty shoes, gratitude prevailed. In fact, it is the acts of unexpected kindness, like the aunt who helped her pick out her wedding dress, that she chooses to remember with appreciation.

Now maybe my parents fell in love because they happen to live near each other and have mutual friends. But it's also possible that it was this common value of gratitude that made my parents destine for each other.

My upbringing was also filled with messages and examples of all variety of service and generosity. Whether by giving to the poor (though I'm not sure we weren't poor ourselves), to going to hospitals during a Clown Ministry phase, my parents were always involved with the doing of kindness. The messages that underpinned these acts were similar to my grandmother's: We have so much.

Over the years, they adopted a displaced family, took in troubled teens from an emergency shelter organization, and made us have Soup Wednesdays, giving the money we would have spent on real food to the Medical Missions Sisters. Even now, my mom volunteers at an outreach center, my parents tithe to the church, and they sponsor a Family Christmas Fund where anonymous envelopes of cash are left in the mailboxes of families that are struggling financially.

When I think about my own experience with gratitude, I can appreciate how this trait, like a family heirloom was passed down from generation to generation. And from my own childhood memories, I can see how constantly and purposefully this family trait was nurtured, cajoled, guilted (we were Catholic after all), and expected. Did I always get it? Nope - and honestly I still forget to be grateful more often that I would like. But, as a parent myself now, I truly appreciate how my parents took the time to instill this trait in me.

So it's no wonder that I have tried to impart this practice on my own 3 sons. And I worry that they don't always get it. Of course, unfortunately for them, because gratitude is so inbred in me, it's also my biggest button when I see acts of ingratitude.

And I am concerned beyond my own family. Because while every generation complains about the lack of gratitude of the next, it is possible that this valuable attribute is more of a challenge than ever to pass on to our children. Gratitude, like compassion and empathy, is a slow-growing trait. It needs an environment that nurtures and tends it to insure it's survival. It is possible that these days, with our time-crunches, abbreviated communications, shorter attention spans, and all the noise coming from the screens that we stare at each day, the vital and life-enhancing practice of gratitude may be a dying art.

And I am not alone. Many of the parents that I heard from during my research have similar concerns. They worry that their children act entitled, ungrateful, and callous toward all the benefits that hold them up. They are worried that their kids have little perspective and do not seem to appreciate the abundance, even in these trying economic times, that they live with.

But there is also great cause for hope. Because besides concern, many of the stories I received were both heartwarming and great examples of parents passing on the messages of gratitude to their offspring. I invite you, no matter what your connection to gratitude and children, to contemplate the narratives within these pages, ponder your own gratitude heritage, and to find ideas and energy for passing on or creating new practices of gratitude for the children in your life.

Thanks for caring about gratitude and children, and for reading.

~ Mahalo, Annie Zirkel

Chapter 1
Why Gratitude?

There is not enough room in the human heart for depression and gratitude at the same time.

~ Jason Hall, Author and motivational speaker

How Big A Deal Is Gratitude?

So the title of this book, *You'll Thank Me Later - A Guide To Nurturing Gratitude In Our Children (and why that matters)* is a bit dramatic. Maybe you got this book because you wish your kids would be more appreciative of their birthday presents - you weren't looking to save their souls or anything.

And come to think of it, so what if your kid gets a present and doesn't say, 'thank you?' Or they don't seem to notice many of the deeds their parents do for them. What are reasonable expectations? What if they don't appreciate their grandparents, teachers, coaches, friends? Or they take for granted the benefits they have in their lives like good food, a roof over their heads, decent clothes, opportunities to learn, an iPod®? They're just kids. Is it such a big deal?

Then there are the REAL basics like running water, electricity, a stable government, no bombs going off outside their homes - can you really expect a kid to appreciate these givens in our society? At what point does their lack of gratitude become a big deal?

The Science of Gratitude

When I first started writing this book, my thoughts on this topic came from my own desire to instill gratitude in my children. Contemplating my own childhood experiences, reading, experimenting, and evaluating my children's gratitude abilities and those of their peers led to many of the insights in these pages. As my exploration into this topic continued, I discovered that science had already produced a body of research to back up many of the conclusions I had made from my own observations.

In fact, Robert Emmons in his book, *Thanks: How The Science of Gratitude Can Make You Happier* (2007) sums up this research by stating that:

[G]rateful people experience higher levels of positive emotions such as joy, enthusiasm, love, happiness, and optimism, and that the practice of gratitude as a discipline protects a person from the destructive impulses of envy, resentment, greed, and bitterness. We have discovered that a person who experiences gratitude is able to cope more effectively with everyday stress, may show increased resilience in the face of trauma-induced stress, and may recover more quickly from illness and benefit from greater physical health.

Powerful Implications

Encouraging our children to notice and appreciate those presents, or their teacher, or the nice sandwich you just made them, is the first step to something much deeper.

Besides helping them find more happiness and joy in life, gratitude improves our children's abilities to handle and survive what life throws at them. Asking a child to notice the gifts of stuff, time, resources, interest, attention, and love, is not just an exercise in politeness, but a critical component in raising children who may:

• handle disappointment and rebound quicker
• gripe less
• have more respect for themselves and others

- have more meaningful relationships
- avoid having an entitlement complex (or worse, becoming a narcissist)
- grow up to be more responsible adults
- have a broader perspective about what is and is not important in life

Want your children to like their family and school better? Instill gratitude. It turns out, "children who practice grateful thinking have more positive attitudes toward school and their families." (Froh, Sefick, & Emmons, 2008)

Feeling gratitude toward someone or something outside yourself brings that person or experience to life. It is by seeing the people, situations, and supports that sustain you that you come to understand how you're connected to the world around you. You are reminded that you are part of something bigger, that you're not alone.

And Why That Matters

So why does that matter? If I haven't already sold you on gratitude being an important aspect of a quality life, science has shown a strong positive correlation between happiness, health, and longevity. Unfortunately, the converse is also true - unhappy people are more susceptible to illness, and they live statistically shorter lives. At its extreme, unhappiness slides into the darkness of depression - a serious condition that can gravely impact one's quality of life, and in its worst cases can lead to tragedy.

And while I am not suggesting that gratitude, by itself, is enough to counter the effects of a serious depression, the practice of gratitude can help counter some of depression's symptoms. It is easier to see the glass as half full when you are grateful for the water.

The Pursuit of Happiness

It turns out that gratitude is an overarching trait that leads to happiness and life satisfaction. If you believe happiness is a goal you feel your children (and you) deserve then gratitude may be the key to achieving it. The U.S. Constitution grants us the right to pursue happiness. But pursuing it turns out to be much easier than catching it. One of the best ways of actually catching happiness is through gratitude. That is how important gratitude is! No matter what life hands you - it is gratitude that can save you.

Chapter 2
How Gratitude Grows

Go to foreign countries and you will get to know the good things one possesses at home.
~ Johann Wolfgang Von Goethe, 18c writer

Getting Some Perspective

Speaking of perspective, let's start by getting some ourselves. Parents' frustrations with their children's ingratitude is not a new concept. Possibly from the beginning of time, parents have heaped charges of ungratefulness 'for all we do' on their children. Who knows how many times, cave moms and dads heard, 'What - wooly mammoth again?!'

Back to our times, for the past century or so, the economic progress of Western nations has meant that, until recently, each generation has grown up with significantly greater wealth than the preceding one. This means that each generation of *parents* can fairly easily notice their *children's* advantages. But it doesn't work the other way around. From the child's point of view, there is nothing unusual about their upbringing. They lack the perspective to notice and appreciate their generational advantages.

Of course, when we were kids, we had a similar lack of perspective. While our parents or grandparents had the Depression, most of the post-WW2 generation and beyond, had the basics and then some, when it came to life's creature comforts. Remember, *we* didn't even walk to our unheated, one room school houses, barefoot through the snow, five miles, uphill - both ways. But most of us didn't have nearly as much as our children, and many of us had the benefit of our parents' and grandparents' stories of the Depression and wartime rationing to give us some sense of balance.

Until the most recent economic downturn, many modern children had little experience with deprivation or scarcity. So it is no surprise that kids don't have a good understanding of the big picture.

How Did You Get Perspective?

Think back to your own childhood. Were you always grateful? If you never complained - either out loud or to yourself - that life was giving you a raw deal, then you are truly way ahead of most of us.

If so, how did you get that way? Some people are born with a propensity for positive emotions. You may be one of the lucky ones. Some children start with so little, and struggle so hard for each gain (think Oliver Twist), that they learn the lessons of gratitude out of necessity. Some children are taught gratitude in such a way that the message gets in without the guilt or resentment that can sometimes tag along.

But if you weren't wired that way, felt so needy that any gains seemed too little-too late, got mixed messages about gratitude, or you really were just a regular non-grateful kid - you might have slipped once or twice. Is it possible that you frowned when you got that tacky sweater from Aunt Millie? Perhaps you complained that it was too cold in the house instead of appreciating that you had any heat at all. And just maybe a gripe passed your lips when the Tuna Casserole Surprise landed on your plate rather than being ever so grateful that at least you had something to eat.

A Healthy Relationship With Gratitude

Even if you did feel grateful, you very possibly felt a mix of negative emotions along with it. Gratitude can get tangled up with guilt, resentment, mistrust, shame, a sense of inferiority, feelings of indebtedness, and conflict with the giver. Having a healthy relationship with gratitude is a goal worth striving for, and one to support in our children.

Guilt is one of the most common gratitude-inducing tools that parents use.

In my family guilt seeped in through lecture and forced sacrifice. We heard about the children in Biafra when we complained about what we were having for dinner. Of course Soup Wednesdays posed a double whammy - you couldn't complain because of the children in India that the Medical Missions Sisters where helping AND as a back-up there were the children in Biafra! We did not get a color TV for years because, as my father put it, "It helps remind us of all the people that don't even have a TV set in the first place."

Some of these methods worked better than others. For instance, my response to starving children in Biafra was a mixture of extreme annoyance - "Well lets send them this Tuna Surprise!" - and extreme guilt that children were starving. (In fact, I didn't learn until my research for this book that in 1967, when I was griping about what was for dinner, part of Nigeria had revolted and for 3 years was the country of Biafra. During that time a million people in the region died from the war and starvation). Of course, not having perspective back then, I could be flip with my comments and not go to a place of gratitude. In retrospect, though my parents' intentions were honorable, this was probably not the most successful approach.

Another way to offer perspective is through what I call 'a hard slap.' My husband remembers how his father gave him the - be grateful for what you have no matter what - philosophy. A favorite reply to some childhood complaint was, "It's better than a poke in the eye with a stick." And while I'm pretty sure he's right, this approach doesn't necessarily make it easier to feel grateful in the moment.

This method may succeed, but at an emotional cost. Or it could backfire completely, creating resentment rather than gratitude, especially if that slap comes in the form of a threat, as in "I'll give you something to cry about." While 'the hard slap' can wake children with a start, it also adds a biting message that they should be ashamed that they were having a good life and forgot. Unless the world is extremely challenging on a regular basis - it's unreasonable to expect that kids will have the ability to stay conscious of their advantages at all times.

A third method of encouraging gratitude is to give children a chance to see what life could be like in different circumstances and let them figure it out.

This story from Ellen M. described the occasional road trips her family took:

Sometimes, my father, a firefighter, would pile the whole family in the car and bring us to the site of a house fire he'd battled the night before. Discussions always revolved around compassion for the family who had lost their home, and while there was a twinge of guilt, eventually we were all feeling gratitude for the roof over our own heads and for our warm beds.

The Seeds Of Gratitude

Kids don't automatically have gratitude. It is a trait that must be cultivated. Helping our children's perspectives to grow is a delicate balance. It can only come with seeing bigger and bigger perspectives. But how does someone encourage that?

When our children are small, start with the more tangible opportunities for gratitude - being grateful for the book we just read, the grapes that are yummy, the bug on the sidewalk. As they get bigger, and at a pace that is reasonable for their maturity, we expose them to other possible experiences that they could be having, to give them perspective.

This story, relayed by Marion H. offers a glimpse at her parent's approach to growing perspective.

My parents were never rich; my father was in the military and my mother was a teller in a bank. When I was 9 years old we moved overseas, to Belgium. Down the street from us was an orphanage, and across the street from us was a family with four boys who had a small farm.

My sister and I tried valiantly for weeks to have the boys come over and play with us, but they were never allowed. Finally, my mother went over to find out why. Turned out they had way too much work to do, and did not have free time.

At age 9 and 7, we simply didn't understand this. So my parents did a switch. My sister and I did their work, and they got to be "us" for a week.

It was an eye-opener let me tell you! We were doing chores that we didn't even know existed - gathering eggs, milking a goat, bringing straw / hay to the horses, being chased by geese and ducks because we forgot to feed them first!

We learned a lot about how other people live and how we should be thankful for what we have.

A couple of times a year my sister and I had to clean out our "playroom" and decide which toys, books, etc. we no longer played with. We'd pack them up in boxes and the family would drive down the street to the orphanage and bring the nuns the toys.

The amount of gratitude that we witnessed from the nuns (we never met the children) was hugely profound for a 9 year old. I vividly remember one of the nuns with tears in her eyes because two younger children were giving their no longer used toys to children who would CHERISH them.

Planting Perspective & Watering It

If your children are lucky enough to have the basics covered and then some, and their lives are pretty safe and stable, you have to figure out ways of helping their perspective grow. Children who have no real experience with deprivation, loss, or upheaval, often gripe about fairly petty things due to lack of experience.

So we need to add water and other elements to help our children's perspectives grow. To do that, we may need to look outside of our own homes, families, neighborhoods, or even outside our country to find teaching opportunities.

A paradox to gratitude development is that sometimes the harshest conditions, produce a hardy gratitude that stays with you. This might explain the balanced perspective of many Depression era seniors. You are grateful for a simple meal. You are grateful for not being sick. You are grateful to go to school. What? Kids grateful to go to school? Yup. Read *Three Cups of Tea* by Greg Mortenson and David Oliver Relin for an interesting shift in paradigm that you and your children might appreciate. (Of course don't overwater this point either. But maybe in a good moment when your kids are open to it, ask them if you can read them an interesting passage. Read it and then add - 'pretty wild huh?')

In some cases, we don't have to look far to find challenges. There are people in our own communities, and often our own lives, who are dealing with divorce; illness; stressful home, work or school conditions; and of course the challenges of these economic times. In these cases, gratitude may not need more water, but some shelter so that it can be nurtured. Appreciating, that while these situations are never ones you would wish on someone, finding your way through them may at least give you a larger perspective in which to find gratitude.

Chapter 3
Kinds of Gratitude

Saying thank you is more than good manners. It is good spirituality. ~ *Alfred Painter*

Gratitude is a destination. It is a sensation, a feeling, a thought, an awareness that informs you that you have or are getting something and that that something has a benefit. It is also a perspective, or a choice to notice and frame your experiences in a positive way. It does not depend on what the world gives you - good or bad, more or less - but on how you decide to receive it. When brought to higher levels, it can become a skill, an art, a practice, a way of being, and even surviving.

Stages of Gratitude

The goal of fostering gratitude in children is to help them develop this attribute to higher and higher levels. Like kids, we start at the beginning and as they develop we encourage their gratitude to grow as well.

For younger children, the aim is to encourage levels 1 and 2. As children get older, and their development and perspective naturally evolve, parents can help foster the more complex levels and be ready to give wise counsel for when the world offers it's own gratitude lessons. Here are the stages:

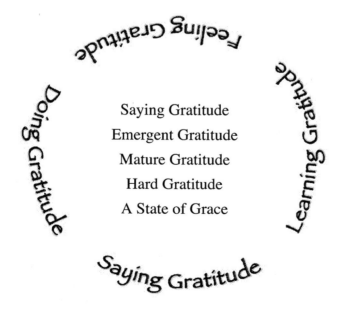

Saying Gratitude
Emergent Gratitude
Mature Gratitude
Hard Gratitude
A State of Grace

Stage 1: Saying Gratitude

Gratitude is more than the act of saying 'thank you' but it is a good place to start. Saying Gratitude is about politeness, courtesy and manners. Both our larger society and most of us, expect shows of gratitude, so teaching politeness is valuable.

Unfortunately, there's good news and bad news about Saying Gratitude.

The bad news is that, first, it is not exactly the same as true gratitude. You can say 'thank you' or write a 'thank you' card without truly experiencing gratitude. Also, some parents teach this level of gratitude superficially, more from a 'What will people think?' motivation than a true appreciation for the concept. Of course if a parent is not in touch with their own deeper gratitude experience they will likely raise children to be the same - raising courteous, though possibly non-grateful, children. The final challenge of trying to teach the saying of thanks is that done with too much pressure or shame, it can backfire, creating children who balk at expressions of gratitude or who may not be open to experiencing true and deeper levels of appreciation.

But luckily, there is good news. Teaching politeness can be a spring board toward internalizing genuine feelings of gratefulness. Modeling, expecting, explaining and teaching the reasons for expressing thanks to others can plant the seeds. Especially when children are younger, this is a good place to start. (For specific suggestions and strategies for developing and practicing Saying Gratitude - see the Appendix). And luckily, if they do mature to higher levels of gratitude, having practice in expressing it will come in handy.

Stage 2: Emergent Gratitude

Learning Gratitude is like learning to read. First you learn what the letters are, then the sounds, then the words - that is what Stage 1: Saying Gratitude is all about. Stage 2: is where you begin to appreciate the meaning of the words. Once you have that down, you can actually learn from what you read.

Emergent Gratitude is when a child begins to tap into their internal gratitude center, and the types of conditions for gratitude begin to expand to incorporate both tangible and intangible experiences. At this level the child's gratitude can be triggered by the external world giving them something or from a noticing of what they already have. Like a switch that gets turned on in a seed, it begins to germinate and sprout. There is an awareness at this stage - a budding force of gratefulness.

Even young children can demonstrate a sense of appreciation through spontaneous, joyous squeals and hugs when given a favorite toy, or when their babbling is correctly interpreted and responded to. However, these seeds need to be nurtured to actually grow into a truer form of gratitude

One way to do this is to narrate these scenarios, highlighting gratitude. "You love this teddy don't you. Aren't you glad we found him under the bed?" or "Oh, you're so happy to be picked up." These kind of narrations - as long as they are accurate - can fertilize the soil for gratitude.

With very young children, tangible benefits will be easier to process than intangible ones. The easiest scenario to see gratitude is when you get something <u>physical</u> that you really wanted, were not necessarily expecting, and did not already feel entitled to. Let's say a new toy that you instantly love. But assisting a child in seeing intangible acts of kindness and generosity is essential to growing their gratitude capabilities.

As children get a little older, pointing out some of the moments when the world gives them things or holds them up helps our children appreciate those around them. An awesome example of putting words to deeds was submitted by a mom, Gail E. When a 'teachable moment' occurred, she would comment with statements like:

- *"Did you see how that woman gave up her seat for that pregnant lady - what did you think about that?"*
- *"What is the name of your bus driver? Isn't it nice that she gets up so early every morning to get you to school?"*

You can also point out the kindnesses of your children:

- *"That lady behind the counter looked like she was having a really bad day - I'm glad you made her smile."*

Expressing genuine gratitude at this level shows that the seed has begun to sprout. It's growth depends on the conditions of their environment, and the hardiness of the seed to adapt. With good nurturing and some luck it will hopefully continue to grow into even deeper sensations of appreciation.

Stage 3: Mature Gratitude

Mature Gratitude is the ability to experience a deeper connection to the world, the wherewithal to withstand and even flip situations where gratitude does not seem to be the logical response, and the grounding of being ok or feeling full and content with what you have.

It is about counterbalancing disappointment, keeping your expectations low (even if your hopes are high), and being big enough to reduce feelings of ingratitude to momentary states.

While modeling and teaching are important to helping children develop Mature Gratitude, much of this level of gratefulness can only come with enough life experience to have a big enough perspective to appreciate what you already have and to not get uptight with 'small stuff'.

Mature Gratitude often develops when what your world offers is pain or loss - divorce, loss of friendship or the death of someone close to you, or any of the hundreds of ways we are given the lesson that 'life isn't fair'. To be able to find a place where gratitude can balance disappointment - when your child has that skill down (or when we have that skill down) - we have the answer to life!)

For this skill to be modeled well, an acknowledgment first of the disappointment is important. This is not about denying loss, but of learning to appreciate loss in a bigger context. But remember children start out little so what we might see as a little disappointment - say the loss a melted ice cream cone or the loss of a soccer game - may be a big disappointment, relative to their size. Acknowledging what they aren't getting, or what they lost, with empathy before we hurry them along to get over it - is actually a better way of fostering children to bounce back and will often help them find their gratitude faster.

If life does not offer enough of its own lessons, parents need to find ways of bringing in messages that help grow a child's perspective. Examples of what some parents do to encourage this level of gratitude include: discussions about the world to give the 'fairness question' a larger context, community service, reading stories or watching programs that depict families with difficulties, or creating situations of purposeful sacrifice that can offer a glimpse of others' life journeys. (See Chapter 8 for more ideas.)

If children don't have many experiences to grow their perspective organically, this level of gratitude may bloom later, bearing fruit only when they are more exposed to the world and see what they had for the first time.

Going away to college can be an eye-opener and I have heard from many parents about the differences in gratitude from their children when they return after the first year away. Getting out into the work world, and seeing how it operates outside of the home can also trigger more sophisticated levels of appreciation.

And of course, how many of us truly appreciated our parents before we experienced parenting ourselves? Sometimes gratitude takes a long time to mature. (Seriously - thanks Mom and Dad!)

Stage 4: Hard Gratitude

Hard Gratitude can only come from living with hard life experiences. Some examples include families with regular or daily challenges such as a member in chronic pain, dealing with constantly unstable work or housing issues, being the primary caregiver of a grandparent or child with limitations, or living in abject poverty. In these circumstances, an attitude of gratitude (and a decent sense of humor!) can make all the difference.

But hard circumstances don't automatically inspire gratitude. You still have to choose to notice and appreciate the gifts, no matter how small. Taking gratitude from the maxim: What doesn't kill you makes you stronger - can be a place to start.

What gets a person to choose gratitude in trying circumstances? People who practice Hard Gratitude do so because they know that gratitude is one of the few choices they still have.

As the mother of a severely disabled son myself, I know this first hand:

My oldest son, Alex, is severely disabled. He is dependent on a wheelchair, and cannot feed, dress or toilet himself. He lacks the ability to talk and is optimistically the developmental age of a 2 year old. He relies on us for everything from changing him, to moving his wheelchair, to bathing him and finding meaningful things for him to do all day. He needs 24/7 monitoring, catches just about every bug that comes through, has a variety of physical conditions - like aspiration that makes him prone to lung infections, and scoliosis that will likely require surgery one day.

And while all that is true, these are just the facts and don't offer even the remotest picture of who he is.

Here are just some reasons I am grateful for him:

He is the most simply pleaseable. Just sing a silly song, or turn on music and he is so joyous that he 'sings' along with you. He is the most loving, loyal, forgiving person I have ever met. He holds no grudges even when we aren't very quick at getting up with him in the middle of the night. As soon as my husband or I enter his room, his complaining turns to grinning at his gratefulness of his ability to summon us.

His innocence and pure goodness can teach the most 'intelligent' leaders of the world a thing or two. He is where I go when the world feels harsh or I am feeling unsuccessful in life. He has forced me to grow in ways I cannot imagine ever doing had I not had to deal with his limitations. My acceptance, my creativity, my spirituality, my parenting, my muscles - all strengthened because of my son Alex. And while - it really is a hard daily life - physically taking care of another person - I am so eternally grateful for him.

Even his brothers would agree. In writing this book, I asked my second oldest son, Adam, if he thought we had helped him learn gratitude and if so - what did we do right? His verdict? He gave most of the credit to his brother Alex.

Post Traumatic Enlightenment

Not everyone with challenging circumstances can find a way to convert this rocky terrain into a place for gratitude. But many people rather than collapsing in adversity, actually can find a new and more deeply felt purpose and strength. Dr. Rich Tedeschi, a professor of psychology at University of North Carolina identified a condition he labeled, Post Traumatic Enlightenment to help identify people who used their circumstances as an opportunity to find new meaning and gratitude in life.

Post Traumatic Enlightenment is the opposite of Post Traumatic Stress Disorder. It is finding gratitude in life after a serious life altering incident, illness or injury. "They know now, based on what they've been through, how tough things can be."

And while shock and anxiety are natural immediate responses to trauma, Post Traumatic Enlightenment often develops for many as contemplation to answer the question of 'Why' sets in. Research has found that for many people– perhaps even most people, life ultimately becomes richer and more full of gratitude.

Stage 5: A State of Grace

Very few people reach this level of gratitude. It can happen only under extremely challenging circumstances and needs the somewhat inhuman strength to stay grounded to gratefulness despite it all. It is a pureness of heart. And though certainly not an essential ingredient, many people reach it because of a faith in God or a higher power.

Like Patricia Fragen, you may have had the opportunity to experience this first hand:

During my daughter's two years of treatment for cancer up until her actual death, at age 16, she never ceased to be grateful for the "cool things" in life. How did she learn it? Honestly, I think part of it she came into the world with, but the balance was reinforced through a lot of community service projects that we did together starting at a very young age and repeated encouragement to use every new experience for learning & growth - thus appreciating each moment for what it provides, whether blissful joy or a harsh lesson to help us in the future.

Today, Patricia has a not-for-profit helping parents with critically ill children.

You will never find more grateful human beings than these folks and their children. It would be good for people to learn gratitude without having to go through the atrocity of critical childhood illness, however that is another way that people quickly learn to appreciate the "normal moments" life has to offer.

Others who have reached this level may find their way either because of their upbringing or despite it. A person who is abused in horrific ways or who losses a loved one in a brutal manner, and yet is able to stay above bitterness and resentment, find forgiveness and cling to their gratitude are examples of finding a State of Grace.

Imagine a person unfairly imprisioned for a long period of time for a crime he did not commit, yet choosing not to be bitter over the time they lost and focus instead on their belated freedom. Nelson Mandela exemplified this after his release from prison after 27 years in 1990. He chose to fight for reconciliation rather than revenge - that is a State of Grace.

Another example is Randy Pausch. A college professor dying of cancer, Randy offered up his Last Lecture and his last few months on this earth to spread the message of gratitude and challenge others to appreciate every moment.

The reason we are awestruck when we hear of these stories is because we doubt our own ability to reach such a state. But the good news is that, whether by hearing these tales or being in the presence of these amazing people, sometimes their grace is contagious. And by staying in touch with your gratitude you are that much more ready if you ever find yourself in the position of needing grace.

As children are able to absorb information about some of the tougher challenges in life, reading about some of the more dramatic stories can give them pause. Accounts of the lives of icons such as Anne Frank, Mother Teresa or, for older children, Viktor Frankl's descriptions of life and death in a concentration camp in Nazi Germany, in Man's Search for Meaning give opportunities to inspire children to raise their sights. And give them new perspective for appreciating their own lives.

In A Nutshell - Let's help children with:

- Life is great
- Life is fine
- Life is still fine
- Life could be worse
- Challenges can teach me great lessons
- My grief today is a testament to the amount of joy I have already experienced
- Gratitude is a choice, and maybe my only one

Finding The Balance

Wanting things and being grateful for what we already have is a delicate balance. Dissatisfaction can be energizing for us to obtain success. And not speaking up for yourself if you are being taken advantage of is not a good trait to instill in our children either. There is a balance.

Gratitude, Nongratitude & Ingratitude

In Robert Emmons' book, *Thanks! How The Science of Gratitude Can Make You Happier* he discusses the difference between gratitude, non-gratitude and ingratitude. We discussed what gratitude is earlier in this chapter. Now let's take a look at his work to clarify a concept that parents should be equally aware of.

There is a difference between a child (or grown-up) being non-grateful as opposed to that child expressing ingratitude. Being non-grateful is about not noticing or acknowledging gifts and kindnesses or not reciprocating the kindness. Expressing ingratitude is about actually putting down the gesture by either criticizing the gift, dismissing or challenging the motive of the giver, or reciprocating with UNkindness toward them. These distinctions should be recognized when examining the state of your child's gratitude level.

Is your child just not aware of the world that holds them up? Or are they actually hostile to these supports. When looking at children (and grown-ups) with an entitlement complex there is often a balking at acknowledgement toward the giver that can be expressed quite contemptuously even while wanting the benefits that the giver is providing.

Gratitude Is An Attitude

It isn't just how much you get. It is where you put your focus. I have seen people get little and be grateful - understanding that getting something is better than getting nothing. But I have also seen people get support and instead of noticing what they are getting, they want to know what's next. It's a bottomless pit on need.

After Hurricane Katrina hit in 2005, I went to Mississippi to volunteer for the Red Cross. I saw people who had lost everything be given many items and emotional support from a community that had taken them in their own make-shift shelter. Many of the evacuees spent much of their time in a place of gratitude - grateful that they were alive, grateful that they were with family, grateful of the outpouring of support. While others never said thank you for anything, complained about their lives and wanted to know what else was coming. And while some of the giving certainly fit into the category of questionable motives, much was truly given from the heart.

My thoughts were that for some of the shelter residents, this was one of a lifetime of hurricanes that had swept through their lives and gratitude had never had an opportunity to be planted, let alone nurtured.

Teaching Children Ingratitude

On the flip side of INgratitude as a negative state of being, I believe that there are times where ingratitude is the correct response. Not every motive behind giving is genuine, and not all acts of kindness are actually kind.

Like in the case of some of the gestures after Hurricane Katrina, at times there were unspoken agendas. In one instance, the church group that provided a meal, then asked a resident to pose with them for a picture holding the sandwich pretending to take a bite - like this shelter was a tourist attraction, and the shell-shocked shelter resident was a sideshow. How much gratitude should this person have mustered? (For more on this see How To Be A Good Giver in the Appendix.)

As the saying goes, 'If it seems too good to be true it probably is'. When someone offers something, part of a child's growth is to assess how genuine the gesture is. To take all acts of giving and kindness at face value is not reasonable because not all acts are pure and unconditional. Helping a child hold on to, and continue to develop their gratitude, also involves helping them decipher whether, and to what extent, a situation warrants gratitude.

The flaws of parents come to mind. Not everything a parent does is - um - perfect. Sometimes far from it. As a therapist, I spend some of my time helping people decipher their childhoods - in part to help clients appreciate the difference between a parent's love and a parent's ability to give their child what he or she needed. Appreciating that parents try, and appreciating that they didn't always get it right is an important distinction and one that can lead, not only to a person's healing, but often to better parenting of the next generation. As parents, when we help our children learn to distinguish what merits gratitude, it gives them a huge head start.

The good news is that while a child can't cherry pick the parts of his or her parents that work, there are still opportunities for gratitude. First, most parents get enough of it right so that kids are grateful for them. But even with the weaknesses - in many cases, as children survive them, they gain a strength to be grateful for.

It helps when parents are able to apologize for the parts of the package that did some damage. Not with self-loathing but with empathy for your child. And of course, chances are that the baggage they passed on traveled a long way itself - inherited from older generations of parents, down through ages. But hopefully, if the luggage isn't too damaged, you and your children can find genuine ways to connect and continue a grateful journey together.

Chapter 4
Challenging Conditions for Gratitude

Most human beings have an almost infinite capacity for taking things for granted. ~ *Aldous Huxley, 20th century writer and author of A Brave New World*

If you are frustrated at your children's lack of appreciation, you may want to consider what conditions are working against their ability to grow gratitude. Some are forces of nature, and need to be understood so that our expectations are reasonable. Some are forces of our society and are, to an extent, beyond our control. Some are forces of nurture and may need to be rethunk on our end. Chapters 4, 5 and 6 will address these issues one at a time.

You Can't Make Me

So let's just get this out of the way. You actually can't make someone else feel grateful. You can guide, and model and expect, offer perspective and attempt to influence gratitude development in many ways BUT genuine gratitude has to come from the inside. If they are capable of gratitude, then it is a choice of the person - and keeping sight of that is quite possibly the most important point to remember for those trying to teach it.

Development and Our Expectations

But first let's make sure that your child actually has a choice. When considering what might be getting in the way of your child's expressions of gratitude, check to see if your expectations are in line with their capabilities.

Power struggles aren't always power struggles. Sometimes you are expecting behavior that your child is not mature enough to display. If teaching and gentle guidance aren't working, then you are either expecting too much of your child or some other aspect of your relationship has interfered with his or her ability to show gratitude (see Chapter 6 for Relationship Challenges).

As stated in Chapter 3, even babies can express joy and happiness as the world responding to your needs is the seed that awaits germination so it can grow into gratitude.

From here the journey takes children to the beginning of seeing themselves as separate from others. 'By age 2 or 3, children can talk about being thankful for specific objects, pets, and people,' says M. J. Ryan., in the book Attitudes of Gratitude. "And by age 4 many children can include intangible acts of kindness as well." But with all skills at this age - if you get 50% success - you are doing fabulously and should be grateful for that! Young children just aren't that consistent.

Toddlers and preschoolers are egocentric - meaning they think of the world as revolving around them. We can work to begin to help them see others, but developmentally they cannot appreciate this concept at a conscious level. As discussed in the previous chapter, this is when you can work on Saying Gratitude - manners - and verbalizing for them some of the many experiences that support them. But be gentle with them. They live in the here and now and gratitude is, in many ways, about seeing the bigger picture.

Dr. Patricia Nan Anderson in her book *Parenting: A Field Guide*, comments:

A parent should not expect a child to exhibit gratitude or appreciation on his or her own before the age of 4... and maybe even later.

A parent can prime the pump, though, at any age. Modeling gratitude and appreciation encourages the kind of reflection needed to understand one's own feelings ("I'm feeling happy!") and the causes of those that lie in the external world ("I love being at the zoo!" or "Aunt Sula was nice to me!"). So a parent can explicitly say, "Wow, that was fun! I'm happy, aren't you? It was nice to be able to play at the playground with other kids.

When your children move toward double digits and beyond, it becomes more of an issue when gratitude does not begin to take root. This chapter may help you pinpoint some of the reasons it may not be developing, but again having reasonable expectations is crucial. If your children have had little exposure to challenges and scarcity and you have not helped open that perspective to them in ways that are effective, expecting them to 'get it' may not be reasonable. Nan Anderson recommends that:

"Parents of older children would do well to focus on the experience not the outcome. For example, instead of focusing on the score of a soccer game, focus on how much fun it was to play. Kids lose their ability to appreciate their daily experience if all their daily experiences come with an evaluation."

And of course, when your children become adolescents, both rebellion and returning to a developmentally normal stage of self-centeredness, will create a new challenge for both you and your child. Yet despite this, it should be said that some of the overly self-absorbed nature of teens in our culture does not have to be a given. Pushing this a bit and challenging your teens to keep one foot on grateful ground will help them stay connected to this trait. Community service, working for their perks, and insisting on respectfulness when they do ask for your support can help keep the scales more balanced. Explaining that gratitude is not a gift they give others, so much as a gift they give themselves can help.

Adaptation

Another challenge for children and grown-ups is our natural tendency to lose sight of our advantages. You might think that the more you have, the easier it should be to notice, but it doesn't work that way. According to Sonja Lyubomirsky, in her book *The How of Happiness*, because of a phenomenon called hedonic adaptation, people have a natural tendency to become accustomed to a situation or environment and in some ways taking it for granted.

Try this for yourself: Picture yourself suddenly dropped in to a beautiful home on a mountain ridge overlooking the blue green waters of Hawaii. The home is spectacular. You have a pool and a view to die for.

- You walk around soaking in the beauty. You unpack your bags, set out a nice meal, relax on the lanai as warm sweet breezes blow past your face, as you enjoy a spectacular sunset.
- The next day, you wake up, hardly believing your good fortune. You wander lazily back to the lanai and breathe a sigh of wonder. You spend the day exploring your retreat, taking a dip in the pool. Basking in the warm sun. You unwind, relax, and appreciate your good fortune.
- The next day you do the same thing.
- The next day you do the same thing.
- The next day you do the same thing.
- The next day you wonder a little less.
- The next day you sit a little shorter.
- The next day you skip the pool.
- Then next day you nod out the window.

At what point do you lose your gratitude for the view and the beautiful surroundings?

Of course in this situation it might take a while. But it will happen. It is hard to hold on to gratitude. Being appreciative of what you have, when you have it all the time, is challenging. It slips through your fingers because even beauty can become a habit.

Overstimulation

My wise youngest son, Nicky, commented as I was writing this piece, that most kids get so much that it's really hard to remember it all. This is often true. It is hard to pay attention to your appreciation for the comforts and luxuries of an abundant world when every time you turn around a new gift is being bestowed upon you.

If you, the parent, notice a lack of gratitude, too much attitude, and an increase in entitlement in your children, the first thing to do is look around to see whether the giving has been overdone recently.

Holidays, indulgent vacations to Disney, a special party, attention and gifts, can overstimulate a child and bring about the opposite of gratitude. Too much of a good thing is often not a good thing.

But what to do about it? Very nicely cut back, explaining why. "I'm thinking that maybe it's hard for you to appreciate all you have because there has been so much lately. So for today, we going to be giving and not getting."

You would think that this would create a huge complaint from children, but very often after the initial protest, many children actually settle down. Like an overly tired baby who just can't soothe themselves to sleep, sometimes ingratitude is really overstimulation and our children need us to step in and eliminate some of the noise.

The Nature? of Boys

According to research, girls seem to access gratitude easier and with a broader scope than boys. How much of this is biological and how much is cultural is hard to say but it is likely both. Research has even found that American men value gratitude less than men of other cultures. The theory is that gratitude means that A.) You didn't do it alone. Maybe you even needed help. and B.) You are now indebted to someone. Perhaps these messages go against the expectation of the 'self-made man'.

In one experiment, researcher Todd Kashdan of George Mason University discovered that "while women felt greater levels of gratitude when given gifts, men reported feeling burdened and obligated to return the favor. The way that we get socialized as children affects what we do with our emotions as adults," said Kashdan. "Because men are generally taught to control and conceal their softer emotions, this may be limiting their well-being."

And it isn't just men who may struggle with appreciating appreciation. 20th century writer, Dorothy Parker is quoted as saying, *"Gratitude is the meanest and most sniveling attribute in the world."*

Chances are, if you are reading this book, you are not of this frame of mind. But, especially if you have sons, you may want to discuss gratitude more deeply to explore whether any of these messages are getting in.

Being Indebted Can Feel Demeaning

Besides gender as a factor in gratitude, there may be other reasons to reject gratefulness. If you are in a place in your life where you don't have much to offer - such as a child, a needy new parent, a chronically financially-strapped family, or someone who just don't have much clout in the world - being on the receiving end of support can feel unpleasant.

Generosity is charity and can feel demeaning and even reduce your self-esteem. One way of coping with this is to not accept the gift. Which can feel hurtful to the giver and isn't always an option. Another reaction may be to accept but minimize the gift. It's using ingratitude to protect your self esteem.

Having this kind of relationship with giving may help explain some of the perplexing reactions many volunteers reported when volunteering with the Red Cross after Hurricane Katrina. Chronic neediness may feel so discouraging that ingratitude is the result.

The Village We Live In

And then we have the people in our village.

Possibly because of this indebtedness factor or possibly because society has opposing expectations of receiver and giver - teaching children gratitude can be filled with mixed messages.

In our culture, while gratitude for gifts is expected, modesty for giving is equally valued. This can get confusing as family members and others in the community appear to thwart your attempts when instructing your child to say 'thank you' for a kind gesture. For whichever reason, many people respond by letting your child off the hook with an "Oh that's OK.", or "It was nothing" which makes teaching this skill harder. (FYI: Here's a better answer: "You are very welcome.")

And beyond not getting in the way of parent's efforts to instill gratitude practice in their children; teachers, coaches, neighbors, family members, and parents of your children's friends need to consider pitching in as well.

Because parents voices are often relegated to 'blah, blah, blah...' without the message that gratitude is important coming from others as well it will be harder to reinforce. Having other people have expectations of gratitude tells a kid that it's important. It takes a village to grow a grateful child. (Just as long as your village watches the shame. For more on this see Chapter 6.)

Questionable Conditions

However sometimes the world sends backwards messages about gratitude that can warp a child's natural logic. And these are times to make gratitude small and harness ingratitude to change your circumstances. Here are some examples of the messages that all of our children should be hearing from the adults in their world:

- You should not be grateful and accepting of any kind of abuse - physical, verbal, sexual, emotional. This is not love, and you do not deserve it. They should not be appreciative to get hit only once instead of twice. Though you may feel grateful when it is not worse, this is not the way you should have to learn gratitude.
- You should not be grateful that you get a drop of love or kindness in between the abuse or neglect - You should get gallons of it!

- You should not be grateful that you are being bullied at school even if you decide that being bullied is better than being ignored.
- You should not be grateful for prejudice, bigotry, sexism or marginalization of who you are because of a trait that you possess.

These are times to speak up. These are times to say - 'I deserve better than this!' and get support against unfair and unreasonable conditions. At the very least, we need to help our children appreciate that while life may not be fair, in some cases it should be much fairer!

Later on, looking back, surviving these conditions can be a way back to gratitude. Not for the conditions but for the surviving. The strengths you needed to endure can all be counted in your gratitude column. It is possible that these conditions may even prime you to appreciate better circumstances - such as real love, respect instead of bullying, equality instead of discrimination, and the acceptance of you and your voice.

Chapter 5 - Living In A Material World
Market Forces and Gratitude Challenges

Be thankful for what you have and you will end up having more. But if you concentrate on what you don't have, you'll never, ever have enough. ~ *Oprah Winfrey*

The Nature of Our Society

In many ways, our society is not supportive of positive parenting objectives. Not only does it often not value this role, but in some cases, it actively works against parents trying to raise reasonable, cooperative, grateful children.

Take the multi-BILLION DOLLAR massive marketing machine that drives consumers to buy-buy-buy. The goal of advertising is to get you to focus on what you don't have instead of the messages of gratitude which draw your attention to what you DO.

And think about this: When you have people whose jobs depend on whether they can get your kid to tell you that she or he wants that doll, video game or sneaker, you can bet that they will take that task seriously.

Which means parents need to as well. Because while adults should be able to tell when they are being sold something so that they can consciously decide whether they want to buy it, children are more vulnerable. Until we teach our children to understand the goals of commercials and cross-marketing, they will be more susceptible to these strategies.

Why teach gratitude?

Grateful individuals place less importance on material goods; they are less likely to judge their own and others success in terms of possessions accumulated; they are less envious of others; and, relative to less grateful persons, are more likely to share their possessions with others.
- Research finding Emmons & McCullough

Teaching your child to be, at times a non-consumer, and at other times a savvy consumer is a responsibility that parents need to incorporate into their 'to-do' list. The good news is that teaching gratitude can help you do that.

Too Much Giving!

Teresa de Grosbois, author of A Present's Present, shares: *One concern with lack of gratitude that a lot of parents talk to me about is that kids start attaching their happiness to the wanting or having of stuff. So as soon as the stuff disappoints in any way or is broken, their happiness goes out the window. Gratitude sets the foundation for children to understand that happiness comes from within and is therefore in our own control.*

Like love, you can't buy happiness, but that doesn't stop most of us from trying. Are you a human ATM machine with an unlimited bank account? Do your children get every toy, gadget, and latest fad with barely a whimper? Do they have so many possessions that they can't keep track, or can't help stepping on and breaking them? When they have a case of the 'gimmies' do you give in?

In our attempts to show how much we care for our kids, we may be taking the wrong path. Lavishing our children with whatever their hearts desire will not get them to happiness. To give our kids the best shot at that, we need to not give to our kids so much. And it starts early. Mom, Gloria L. shares:

The first 3 years of my twins' lives I gave them everything they wanted because I didn't want them to feel the pain of want that I felt often as a child. I remember the day I realized that giving my children stuff all the time was a bad idea.

When my twin girls were 3 years old, I purchased little dolls from McDonald's as a surprise.

But when I gave them the dolls, to my surprise and disbelief they threw the dolls at me and said. "we don't like these".

From that day forward I changed my ways. I set up rewards systems, and just plain work-for-what-you-want scenarios. They have to earn things they wanted. I no longer gave them whatever they wanted all the way through the grocery line - not even gum. We began sorting through and giving away their unused toys and clothes every year and we began doing service work. I have talked about, and continue to have conversations about, the meaning of gratitude.

. *That was a long seven years ago, and though maybe they are not as grateful as I would like them to be, I do hear them conversing with each other about how lucky they are to have the things and people they have in their lives. So I figure I must be doing something right.*

Watch What You Want

If you find your children griping too much and being grateful too little, you may first want to look in the mirror. If you regularly get caught up in talking about the next thing you're going to get, and treating yourself to impulse purchases, what message are you sending?

Here are two good dinner conversations to try with your children, elementary-aged and up:

1. What's the difference between 'I need' and 'I want'?

2. When is enough, enough?

Therapist Bette Alkazian shares these thoughts about how parents need to notice, and possibly alter, their own comments about stuff:

Kids are little sponges watching their parents. If parents are constantly focused on getting things and discussing the next car, the next electronic gadget, etc., kids may also learn to always yearn for more and never feel satisfied. Talking about how lucky we are to have what we have is a wonderful way to teach kids gratitude.

De-emphasizing Material Gifts

Kelly C., mother of 3, shared her approach to dealing with too much materialism:

One way we hope to help our children to be grateful people is to de-emphasize material possessions in life and to focus instead on relationships and time spent with family and friends.

We strive to steer them away from a sense of entitlement at birthdays by doing a book exchange among all of the party guests so that the focus is not on the birthday child.

Similarly, at holidays, instead of presents, we exchange a special outing among their cousins, whereby our family will host their family for a weekend of fun in our town, and they will do the same on another weekend, emphasizing time spent together, as opposed to a material gift to be enjoyed only by the recipient.

Entitlement

Entitlement is what happens the minute you lose your gratitude. Expectations of getting something for nothing can only develop into an entitlement complex when you get a enough somethings for nothings.

This is another reason to cut back on giving and expect participation and accountability for the getting.

Working For It & Delayed Gratification

When your child says they want something - do you react by hearing that you should get it for them? Instead of saying yes or no - help your children figure out how they are going to get it themselves. Are they going to save their money? Trade with someone? Ask for it for a birthday or Christmas? Or work to get it?

Helping children appreciate the value of money can also cut down on materialism and assist in teaching an appreciation for belongings. Giving them an allowance and having them pay for some of the items that you normally would, can remind children that stuff costs money and that spending money is related to work and choices.

Instant gratification will make it harder for children to appreciate that they have just gotten something. You can help them be more grateful by having them participate in the getting and finding opportunities for them to delay their gratification. Here's an opportunity I unknowingly had to offer this lesson to my children:

When my kids were little there was this promotion on our oatmeal box: Collect and send in 20 empty packets with proofs of purchase and $1, and receive a small alien Lego ® set. My kids had oatmeal coming out of their ears but they finally ate enough to send in our request for two sets. Then we read that we needed to wait 6-8 weeks! I thought they were going to cry but we got out a calendar and marked off the days one at a time. Well 6 weeks later 2 small packages of alien Legos® arrived in the mail. They were so excited! And boy did they appreciate them.

Funny aside was that the next day we received another 2 sets. The day after that it was 10, and the day after that another 8. When I finally found a number to call to see what was going on - it turned out that someone at the distribution center had mistakenly entered 22 sets instead of 2. The company didn't want the toys back, so in the end, all that oatmeal really paid off, and we had party gifts for the next several birthdays.

Too Much Doing

Sometimes it's too much <u>giving to</u> kids, but there can also be too much <u>doing for</u> our kids that gets in the way of teaching appreciation.

Do your children do any of the chores like straightening up, dishes, laundry, taking out the garbage, food shopping, cooking, vacuuming, or house maintenance?

Do they pass the time playing video games, hanging out, waiting to being chauffeured around to their activities, as you run about making sure they have snacks, a clean soccer jersey and all their equipment?

Children will have a harder time learning gratitude under these circumstances. The one word answer? Chores.

Having kids participate to the functioning of the house has an impact on how aware they are of what is involved in moving them through the day. And allows them a much better opportunity to not take that for granted.

It Takes A Village Part 2

Sometimes our village works against us in the gift-giving department. Overly indulgent relatives who insist on giving our children presents that we would rather they not have can make our ability to help our children stay focused on gratitude a challenge.

So what to do? Ask the people in your life to help you teach your child gratitude by cutting back because you want your child to truly appreciate their gifts and too many or too expensive gifts make that harder. Encourage caring relatives to spend more time, not more money - take your child to work, share a community volunteer project together, or expose them to new experiences and learning.

Of course that won't always work. And you may continue to have power struggles with your village, but it is good to lay down your hopes first. After that, your recourse is to insist and return unwanted gifts (hard to do but it may be necessary) or remind your child of your feelings about the downsides to some of these gifts and assist them in their gratitude practice.

Thanking for Non-Tangible Gifts

Helping our kids move from the tangible to the intangible aspects of understanding is part of our job. Especially when you can get them to consider that the really big gifts aren't the monetary ones. How to do that? Help them practice saying 'thank you' for NON-monetary presents.

Gifts of time, attention, kindness, family coming to watch their baseball games, working hard to give them a pleasant home, driving them places, teachers teaching, coaches coaching are all worth big thank yous.

Giving Up - I Mean...Giving It Up

Going without or fasting has a long tradition in many religions. One way to appreciate what you have is to experience what it is like to not have it. But if your life affords you all the necessities and many of its' luxuries, the only way to experience the lack of something is to force it.

If you don't already observe fasting or giving up something for religious reasons, consider doing it as part of your family's quest for gratitude.

When I wanted to teach my kids about hunger we fasted for a day. Actually it was only until dinner, when we ate a small meal. All day we struggled not to gripe about our grumbling stomachs. When dinner came, the meal never tasted so good. It was a small opportunity to remind ourselves of the bounty that we partake in every day.

In fact, it was so worthwhile that we repeated it - only this time 'fasting' from computers, TVs and anything with a screen - the following Sunday. This was such a refreshing change of pace that my husband and I decided to continue it. There are some Sundays that we forget or let it slide, but for the most part we've been able to cut back here, fairly painlessly. (Though my kids might not say that last part.)

Teaching your children the value of money, and balancing their materialism with contentment and an appreciation for what money can't buy will help you raise more grateful children. The added bonus is that by taking this task seriously and doing it well, someday, if they have monetary wealth, there is a great chance that they will do something generous and awesome with it - like buy you a house! No - I'm only kidding.

Chapter 6
Relationship Challenges to Gratitude

Let us rise up and be thankful, for if we didn't learn a lot today, at least we learned a little, and if we didn't learn a little, at least we didn't get sick, and if we got sick, at least we didn't die; so, let us all be thankful. **~ Buddha**

How unfair is this! Pretty much all of parenting lands on the shoulders of the PARENTS! And we have so many opportunities to screw it up.

Unfortunately, besides the abundance and lack of accountability we give to our children, there are other dynamics that may be playing into why our children do not possess more gratitude. Some of these factors have to do with HOW we try to instill it, others include what the condition of our relationship with our children was, in the first place.

Boundaries

Remember that point made in Chapter 4 that you actually can't make a child be grateful. Well they actually can't make you make them their favorite macaroni and cheese dinner either.

Lack of boundaries about what your job as a parent is, versus what you do out of generosity is an important distinction in parenting. Complaining about our children acting entitled or bratty can often be traced back to our behavior when they are in need of our services. Teaching your child good boundaries is a critical aspect of good parenting. And it starts with your own self-respect.

My number one rule in the area of teaching gratitude is that I do not give my children something if they don't seem to appreciate that I have a choice in giving it. If they demand or just expect me to do these extra niceties, I won't. "You have to help me with my homework.", "I can't find my shoes.", "You need to drive me to practice.", "I've got to have this new computer game."

If your child calls from school to say that they left their homework home, having these two rules will help your child with better boundaries (because <u>you</u> are modeling better boundaries). Only consider bringing it if: 1.) You actually have the time without major stress as a result, and 2.) They understand that they are asking you a favor for which you have a choice. Meaning that they ASK you - nicely - and a 'please' might help. If your child dumps their problem in your lap and just expects that you will solve it - then you know you have a boundary issue.

Gratitude is about seeing what the world gives you. Asking them to see you can be the first step to that.

Shame, Punishment and Consequences

The downside to having a great appreciation for appreciation, is that when you are met with ungratefulness or ingratitude, it can easily push your buttons. The trouble with this is that it can overshadow our desire to encourage gratitude and actually set up a downward rather than upward spiral. Instead of just reacting, one option is to reframe why a behavior upsets us. "You know that gratitude is big with me so when you forget to say thanks after spending the night at a friend's it pushes my buttons."

I've talked about watching shame in teaching our children the lessons that we hope they will learn. The trouble with shame is that, while it actually can be effective in changing outward behavior, it comes at a cost to self-esteem and the ability to feel genuine gratitude. And the reality is that changes made due to shame or fear factors are usually superficial and lack buy-in.

Shame can be seen in underlying messages of disappointment, impatience or implications that our children are not up to par. Yelling and punishing our kids for their lack of thankfulness often loses the lesson in the process. What sticks with kids is the anger, and they're certainly not grateful for that.

In thinking about punishment versus consequences the difference is in what the underlying message is. If you appreciate that many of life lessons are learned by making mistakes and that that is ok - then offering consequences to help your child learn something works well - no shame - just the natural or logical result of needing to learn by your mistakes.

If however these consequences have a knife twist to them, then this is about punishment rather than an appreciation for the fact that we all make mistakes.

An example of this came from a regretful parent in one of my classes:

My son had received a check from his aunt for his birthday. I stated that he couldn't have the money until he wrote a 'thank you'. Two weeks later, the check is still sitting on the window sill and no card has been written. The ensuing confrontation went bad when his father, to make a point, ripped up the check in front of our son.

The boy proceeded to run to his room, mad and certainly not thinking about gratitude.

The challenge in this example is that dad's action did not allow a gracious way for his son to learn a good lesson. When the next gift comes along this boy is in a bind. If he writes a 'thank you' he is saying that the way to teach me is to make me feel ashamed for screwing up. Now he may write the next card, but that kind of a push is likely to make gratitude less accessible rather than more. And depending on how tense the relationship is, next time, he may feel he needs to push the issue again just so that you appreciate that you can't make him feel grateful.

How could this have been done differently? Let the consequence of not getting the money, and the embarrassment of having to see Auntie again knowing what happened, make the point. If he doesn't respond to that, his ingratitude is telling you that he is getting too much and you may need to help him balance the scales.

Angela H. used consequences to teach manners to her children while out trick-or-treating. Again, done without shame, this can help children learn the lesson quickly:

We were so concerned by the lack of courtesy and gratitude when we were trick or treating that we created a new house rule: For every house that they did not say: Hello, Happy Halloween and Thank You, we skipped the next house. It took about three houses before the concept kicked in. What's really interesting is that ever since that night, they have been a lot more polite.

Suspicious Agendas

If a relationship feels contentious, good deeds can be met with suspicion and your child may wonder what the hidden agenda must be. Also the good deed can feel like manipulation as in 'now you owe me' or 'now I want something from you.' This complicates the ability to experience gratefulness because the gesture is suspect. (See Being A Good Gift Giver in the Appendix.)

Also, it's important to be in touch with any social pressure you, as a parent, may be feeling about the expectations that come from our own issues with gratitude. Feeling responsible to speak gratitude because you of guilt or shame rather than truly being able to be in a place of gratefulness is not a good foundation for appreciation.

Then there are the eyes. The ones that many parents feel are watching their every parenting move. Judgments, looks of shame, and pressure to meet others' expectations of our children can make us crazy and push us to push our kids too hard.

Besides, manipulation or feelings of inadequacy in parenting, there are several other expectations that may be getting in the way of encouraging gratitude. Minimizing that this is a skill that must be learned, and regressing into believing that they should already know it will be a challenge. If you think this is a thing you can teach once and be done is like planting a garden and figuring that it will grow on its' own.

Balancing expectations with the reality that kids, just like adults, won't always be grateful at the moment of generosity is important. Also consider that the constant message of 'Be grateful', Be grateful', 'Be grateful' can backfire and create a hardening rather than a softening of the heart. WHEN do you expect gratitude? How much time does it take? Minutes, days, weeks, years, a lifetime?

Think about this: When did you truly begin to appreciate how hard parenting was? Doubtful that you had a real clue before you became one. So give your kids some slack. They can't really know, until they know.

Resentment

Sometimes parents' approaches to conveying a 'Be Thankful' message is, in itself, problematic. Statements laden with mixed messages, shame or contempt, can, justifiably trigger resentment and cause a child to become bitter rather than better at gratitude.

This challenge came up for several grown-ups I spoke with when revisiting their own childhoods.

One woman recalled:

My mom did a lot of this kind of "backhanded compliment" which was, I think, intended to teach gratitude. "Well, at least you're not stupid. Well, at least you can spell. Well, at least you're not fat. At least you're not homely. At least you're not a whiner. And so on." These were said with the implication that I might easily have been any of those things, and I should be grateful for my natural gifts. The "at least" always made me wonder what the implied-but-unmentioned bad qualities I did have were.

Contempt was felt by another woman when recounting her mother's approach to teaching gratitude.

I grew up with a "Believe me, it could be a lot worse!" approach to gratitude. This included both guilt (There are children starving in Africa who would be grateful to have liver for dinner!) and fear (something akin to "I'll give you something to cry about"). This did

*not work particularly well for me. I felt more resentment
and shame than gratitude.*

The Pull-Push of Instilling Gratitude

For the most part, helping children grow their
gratitude works best when we pull them kindly toward a
more grateful state by modeling appreciation ourselves, and
by exposing them to opportunities to see the bigger picture.

Ideally we approach gratitude from a generous
place. We appreciate that our children will forget and we
kindly remind them. But sometimes that can feel too slow
and we may feel that they need a more dramatic wake up
call. Sometimes learning comes from the other direction.
Pushing the point a little harder because they seem
particularly out of touch.

The 'That's Not Fair' Comeback

I believe that fairness is a goal worth striving for.
We want a fair justice system, equal access to education,
and equal pay for equal work seems like a reasonable
concept. Of course we all know that fairness is not always
the reality but for most people it is the ideal.

I don't believe parents need to teach children that
life isn't fair so much as be kind when children discover
this for themselves.

This is not always easy to do. When a child is experiencing unfairness it isn't fun. But parents and other adults can get frustrated when the 'fairness' card is played too quickly. Especially when, as grown-ups, we can appreciate the more challenging cases of unfairness that can happen because we've either experienced or heard about serious circumstances of injustice. Given our knowledge, not getting 10 more minutes to play video games is pretty light-weight on the Fairness Scale.

Of course going back to the reality that a child's perspective is only as big as their experiences, opening their eyes to the truth about unfairness is one of those push-pull affairs. There are times to push their awareness (watching the shame) beyond their immediate vantage point, while continuously pulling and inviting them toward a larger awareness of how the world works.

Not sure when to push and when to pull? Consider these three choices:

PULL: If your child has a decent case; you aren't being badgered, berated, or played; and the scales seem particularly out of whack, offering to set things right can be reasonable and pull them in the direction of gratitude.

EMPATHY AND NO MOVEMENT: We can also validate a child's experience while not being able to, or not feeling obligated to change it. 'I know. It's doesn't seem fair that you have to go to bed earlier than your sister. It's just the way it is when you are younger you need more sleep.' (Note: Sometimes, especially when siblings are involved - fair is not really what they want. They want more than their sibling. When this comes up, the key is to address the need, separate from the sibling issue. Not, 'you want more grapes because your sister has more' but 'you would like more grapes'.)

PUSH: If your child is lost in their small sense of fairness you may need to make the point more clearly. One thing I have said when my kids inevitably say some version of, "That's not fair." is "You are right. But from where I am standing, mostly life isn't fair in your favor."

Dealing With Disappointment

One aspect of fostering mature gratitude in our children is honoring, at least initially, their disappointment.

Sometimes parents are in a hurry. Either because they've lost sight of how big a seemingly small sadness is to a small person, or because they feel their own anxiety when their children go to a negative place, they push a little too hard to move their children's frame of mind.

When it comes to appreciating gifts, it can help to acknowledge when some of the giving isn't always on target like when Great Aunt Sally gives your 10-year-old child a coloring book. But this is a great opportunity to appreciate the giver while admitting that the gift wasn't the greatest. One mom writes:

In regard to receiving gifts, I've always encouraged the girls to say "thank you", not because that's the proper thing to do or that someone gave them something, but because that person thought of them. That is the true gift, and it helps the girls say an authentic "thank you", especially when they receive something they didn't like.

Of course, when it involves more emotional disappointment and involves bigger setbacks, allowing time for grief is crucial.

The Pollyanna Story

In the 1913 book Pollyanna, this 10 year old girl plays the Glad Game - turning setbacks and physical ailments into opportunities to be glad about something. In the original story, this strategy worked for Pollyanna because she was innocent and because she modeled playing this game with her own tragic circumstances.

A Chat About Finding Gratitude

What do you do when you get:
➡ a present that you are a bit unsure of
➡ a present that you don't want
➡ an intangible gift. Someone volunteers to coach
so that you can have a soccer team this year
- but the coach is kind of a pain
- and you lose almost every game

However, parents using this technique while not appreciating its pitfalls may find that it backfires. Done well and with good timing (after validating a disappointment and with respect rather than to dismiss a person's plight), may help a child move to a larger vantage point. However, <u>imposing</u> an 'It could be worse' rationale on someone else can easily lead to resistance rather than gratitude.

Disappointment is valid. It is reasonable to take a minute to bounce back. Shutting down sad reactions to losing a game, not getting a treat they were hoping for, or an even larger disappointment cuts off part of your child's experience. Rushing through this and pushing your child to get back to a place of gratitude may make them hold on to their sadness longer, or lose touch with their ability to acknowledge it in the first place. Both outcomes would be too bad. Plus, pushing a child to appreciate how it could have been worse can often cause a child to dig in deeper to how miserable a situation is.

Mom: (walking away from a soccer field with her son after his team lost): Well at least you only lost by one. (You know your child is in a grateful place if he agrees. But if he was noticeably upset, this would be a big leap so soon after the disappointment.)

Son: We should have won that game! If Joey hadn't let them score twice in the last minute we would have won!

Mom: It wasn't that bad. You could have lost 10 - 1. Or it could have been cold and raining like last week. At least you got to play - unlike how it was at the beginning of the season.

Son: I hate soccer!

When disappointment is reasonable - pulling your child to a better place gently, rather than pushing him to 'get there already' is usually a better approach.

Mom: I know you're disappointed that your team lost. How bad do you feel?

Son: Horrible!

Mom: So it was terrible for you!

Son: Yeah - we should have won that game. If Joey hadn't let them score twice in the last minute we would have won!

Mom: I know that was too bad. Of course <u>you</u> did really well! You were great on defense and you even made that one save single-handedly!

Son: Yeah - but I wanted us to win!

Mom: That would have been good. But you played well and really the rest of the team and your coach tried hard too - even though you lost.

Son: Yeah, I know.

This is not exactly gratitude - however, appreciating how he played, how his teammates played, and the coach's efforts is not accessible until the disappointment is dealt with and moved to the side a little so that he can see past it and hopefully find his way to a place of gratefulness.

The AND Factor

You know your child has reached Mature Gratitude when they can acknowledge the disappointment and then find a counterpoint to it. When they are sad or when they didn't get what they wanted AND they know they will be OK you know they've grown in their gratitude.

Of course some of the 'gifts' life gives us aren't kind. AND yet we need to help our children respond to these bigger disappointments and setbacks as well and come back to a perspective that will help them.

Whether it is dealing with a hurtful friendship, getting cut from the team, breaking up with someone, not getting into the college they wanted, dealing with the divorce of their parents, or losing a loved one, allowing time for these experiences to be processed is crucial to helping your children have a vital and reasonable relationship with gratitude. Of course when some time has passed, inviting them to consider gratitude - this was disappointing AND you survived... AND you handled it... AND it could have been so much worse... AND believe it or not, you will get over it - can help them rise above and re-center themselves to a more positive place.

Chapter 7

How To Nurture Gratitude

The trick is in what one emphasizes. We either make ourselves miserable, or we make ourselves happy. The amount of work is the same. ~ **Carlos Castaneda**

Modeling

Modeling both manners and expressions of heartfelt gratitude will help your children learn these attributes better. Modeling involves showing your gratitude and appreciation OUT LOUD so your kids can hear you.

Candace D., has some great examples of how she models gratitude for her son:

My husband and I say 'thank you' to each other all the time and make sure that our son sees it - even the smallest thing, like 'thank you' for bringing home bread from the store for dinner or folding the laundry, etc.

Whenever I ask my son to do something I always follow it up with a 'thank you' - i.e. 'thank you' for putting your books away, brushing your teeth, being so sweet.

Is it working? I felt the most accomplishment as a mom after I handed my young son a cracker on a car trip and he said 'thank you' all on his own, with no coaching needed. He proceeded to say 'thank you' after each and every cracker he received after that.

Appreciate Your Kids

Kids are often put on hold while we get the stuff of life done. As they wait through the 5th 'Just a minute' - thanking them for being patient allows them to see how they have given something. That is what we want them to see in others isn't it?

How about at the grocery or clothes store. They don't want to be there - when they are good about it - you can thank them for being good.

Some parents are afraid of thanking their children, fearing that it will give kids a mixed message about what they have power over. And I agree that kids need to deal with things - I also think it is a bonus in life to be appreciated for what we are doing. This is not about thanking in a way that makes them think they had a choice in whether they came to the grocery store, it's about thanking them for the attitude they brought along with them. Thanking them for going to bed nicely needs to focus on the nicely.

That goes for partners too. If I thank my husband for getting home in time for dinner, I am just validating his efforts. I am not threatened that he will hear it as he's doing me a big favor. (Same for him thanking me for cooking! Him getting home on time is as much of an effort as me making dinner!)

Lisa B. reflected on her gratitude history by fondly remembering her parents' approach.

My parents taught gratitude by modeling. So, my recollection is that they did not say a lot of "SAY thank you" to us but instead said a lot of "thank yous"- to us for things we would do, to each other for all the mundane things like driving and going shopping and making dinner as well as for gifts, and people they/we encountered in the world - thank you to the person in the checkout lane at the grocery store, etc...

Living Your Gratitude

Beyond saying 'thank you' you want the children in your care to see you living your gratitude. One woman's fond memories of her grandmother, speaks to the power of living your gratitude. Amy H. writes:

My grammy was the best parent-figure at teaching gratitude, because she did it in a way that was utterly natural, not forced or cynical or manipulative. She just took us outside into the yard and the garden and showed us how to feed birds, weed strawberries, fertilize baby trees, water plants in a way that was loving. She enjoyed these labors, and I just learned to like them, too. I liked the little maple trees so much because I had helped them grow. I loved the finches because they politely came and ate the seeds I'd put out for them. I Hated the blue jay for chasing the more timid birds away. Grammy and I would sit and watch them, grateful for the birds that came in to her yard, and for the plants that gave us good food to eat.

She taught me gratitude for books by reading them to me with so much pleasure, and teaching us to take care of them. She always put "from Grammy with Love" inside each book she gave us. She was a children's librarian. I was, and am, so deeply grateful for her loving ways.

Self-Advocacy - And Advocacy For Others

One of the best ways to not only remind children of all they get, but to get some appreciation for yourself, is to self-advocate for gratitude.

When things are feeling a little out of balance, I might step up my children's awareness by pointing out some of the things I do. "I must be a nice mom to make you that sandwich just the way you like it." It usually prompts a genuine thank you, and I feel great about getting it.

I've even done it after witnessing an ugly parent-child scene in a store. "That was really terrible that that mom said those mean things to her daughter. I'm glad I don't talk like that to you." "Me too." was my son's grateful reply.

Without this self-promotional step, parents are virtually invisible and much of the caring goes unnoticed. With this step, it reminds our children that they are doing all right. That they are supported and held up in their lives. And it reminds them that it is actually my choice to do these things.

Of course this can be way over done with guilt and pity-seeking. If you do self-advocate watch the martyrdom messages like, 'Look at all I do for you. You're so ungrateful!' The key here again is balance. This isn't about counting every glass of water I get for a thirsty kid, or pointing out every shirt I fold. (Actually - my kids fold most of the clothes in our house - for which I am extremely grateful - Thanks kids!) But once or twice a day, you might make mention of something kind that you, their other parent, a neighbor, a teacher, or even - believe it or not - a brother or sister! - did for them.

Expectations

Modeling and living gratitude, and advocating for the nice things you and others do are two pieces of the puzzle. Having expectations of your children that they also show gratitude is what is needed to make the picture complete.

In my practice, I have heard this complaint from parents: 'I don't know why they seem so ungrateful. We always modeled politeness in our house.' But not expecting politeness and awareness of gratitude <u>back</u> sets kids up for entitlement not gratefulness. Consider these scenarios:

"Michael, a package came for you!" Excited, Michael rips off the paper to find his prize - a new Lego® set from grandma. He plays with it for hours, enjoying, as

Grandma had hoped he would, this special gift. Unfortunately - Grandma doesn't even know if he got it until weeks later when she finally asks her son.

Brenda walks off the field after a soccer game. The coach gathers up the equipment as Brenda races off to her family's car leaving her coach unthanked for her time and effort.

Mom drives Jamil to a friend's house. 3 hours later mom drives back and picks him up. When she tells him it's time to go she get complaining, negotiating and attitude - everything but gratitude.

The end of another school year. Most of the class runs out of the room at the final bell without looking back or thanking the teacher who just spent 10 months supporting these children's learning.

These are all missed opportunities for our children to notice the abundance they receive from those who love and care about them. If children become ungrateful or feel entitled to get things without acknowledgement or giving back - who is responsible for that? Parents and the rest of our society are the ones sending the message of just how important saying 'thank you' really is.

Thanking: Relatives, Teachers, Coaches, friends' parents, the cashier at the supermarket, the man who holds the door for us to walk through, are all great opportunities for gratitude. I take this responsibility seriously.

Once, my middle son had a sleep over party with a gang of his friends. They had a great time. We got them pizza and pop for dinner, video games, snacks and a movie. The next morning I made a nice, big pancake breakfast. Being 12 year old boys they had pretty hardy appetites and ate like pigs.

At the end of the meal the all got up and went downstairs leaving a messy table and not one thank you.

I nicely called them all back upstairs.

Once they were all seated back at the table, I gave them a mini-~~lecture~~ -lesson in gratitude. I told them that I was disappointed that they had missed an opportunity to say 'thank you'. I explained that I wasn't disappointed for me so much as for them. Because all this good stuff happened - and I listed a bunch - and they forgot to notice. Noticing is not just because it's nice for the other person but because it reminds you that you have a lot of great parts of your life. And remembering them specifically is what will help you be happy.

A few hours later when their parents' were picking them up, several of them, without prompting from a parent, said 'thank you' - and it was genuine. One boy - with his mom staring on, jaw dropped in amazement - went on and on thanking me for a list of specific memories that this gang had just created.

P.S. This story got a second life when I shared it with my other son's friends, during a subsequent sleepover. BEFORE their pancake breakfast was over, I told them about the disappointing manners of some other boys who had visited our house. As younger siblings often do, they got the benefit of the lesson without having to go through the original ordeal.

On The Other Hand

Towering over our children like guards - pointing out ever missed opportunity is not reasonable. And of course, investing in a decent relationship with the recipient of your words of wisdom BEFORE you offer your advice can make a huge difference.

Start with empathy that because your children are engaged in the moment, they may not be thinking of gratitude - a concept that one cannot see. Expecting them to appreciate every gesture is not only unfair but it can inhibit the very wonderful aspect that children are so much better at than most adults - enjoying the moment.

If you appreciate gratitude as a developing awareness, just as your parenting is a work-in-progress, it might help you both. Cindy S. shares and experience she had as a child that she will never forget:

Down the street from where I grew up lived a widow in a very large house, named Mrs. Shaw.

On some spring holiday, my friend and I picked some flowers and headed over to Mrs. Shaw's to give them to her. When we knocked at the door, her housekeeper answered it, thanked us, told us to wait a minute, and took them to Mrs. Shaw who was in another room. The housekeeper came back and handed us a ten dollar bill! We were so shocked that we just took it and got out of there.

When I told my mother about this, she insisted that I go back and return the money. I remember her saying, "you gave this as a gift and you don't take money for gifts." Very reluctantly since I didn't know Mrs. Shaw at all and wasn't sure what to expect, I returned to her house to return the money. I told the housekeeper why I was back and wanted to return the money - that the flowers were a gift - we weren't selling anything. She said to wait a minute, talked to Mrs. Shaw, and then invited me in.

I sat with Mrs. Shaw and had tea in her "parlor"! It was fabulous! I felt so grown up and welcomed. I know that Mrs. Shaw was touched by my effort. I returned probably about half a dozen times to visit with her. I always admired my mom for making me go back.

Finding A Balance Again

Finding a balance between modeling, expecting and holding our children accountable is a step-by-step process. Appreciating that steps backwards are going to happen, and that in the moment - gratitude may not be forthcoming is a good approach.

The key to knowing whether your child is 'getting it' is to check in with them later. Can they express gratitude in retrospect? If not, that's where to start. But if they can, then the goal is to work with them, moving that appreciation closer and closer to the moment that triggered the feeling. And when it comes out spontaneously - not just the words but the experience of gratitude - you know the seeds have taken root and are growing.

Chapter 8

Ideas for Practicing & Doing Gratitude

The hardest arithmetic to master is that which enables us to count our blessings. ~ Eric Hoffer

There are times that we might miss an opportunity for gratitude. That's fine - we don't want to be neurotic about it. But there should be a consistent expectation that as our children grow, their understanding and appreciation for those who hold them up grows with them.

The Big Conversation & Booster Shots

One of the best ways to teach gratitude is to not just do it but talk about HOW and WHY we do it. So the first thing on your list is to have the Big Conversation with the purpose of getting your thoughts about gratitude on the record and checking in with where your kids are.

Include in the discussion both manners and feelings of gratitude and the importance of both. When talking about manners make sure you explain WHY we do this, WHAT our [reasonable] expectations of our children are, and HOW to say gratitude - including role playing if necessary (see Appendix for tips on Saying Thank You).

For children, elementary-aged and older, move the conversation to the broader understanding of gratitude as a state of mind, including being aware of intangible gifts as well as being grateful and content with what you have and even keeping your gratitude when you are faced with disappointments.

Throughout your parenting career, booster conversations will be needed as kids keep growing. Of course - this is when our kids will notice that we don't always say 'thank you' or seem grateful ourselves (and if they're right, we should own it and nicely kick ourselves in the butt as well.)

Finding Gratitude Inspiration

Reading books, watching shows and movies, and spotting exchanges in real life can trigger gratitude teaching moments. These opportunities can also be a great way to keep the conversation going. (See Gratitude Resources list in Appendix for books that can help.)

Pointing out an ingratitude of someone else can also be powerful in showing your children what you hope and expect. "Wow, that girl got her mom to buy her candy at the counter and she didn't even say 'thank you'. Hmph." A word of caution to use this sparingly.

Prayers & Gratitude Rituals

13th century philosopher, Meister Eckhart said it well. "If the only prayer you said in your whole life was, thank you, that would suffice." Whether at bedtime, during the family meal, or at Thanksgiving, the ritual of speaking gratitude can form the foundation of fond family memories.

Mom, Karen T. shared this tidbit: *My middle son asked me tonight, "Mommy, why do you always pray so long?" I replied, "Because I have a lot to be thankful for, many others to pray for, and I hope you'll fall asleep knowing I'm praying for you and our family." No further questions! :-)*

Mother, Meg C. gives grace an unusual humorous twist: *I tried to set an example for my kids by expressing my thankfulness verbally for our family, health, education, opportunities, and stuff we have. I would regularly thank the cow at dinner for the meat she gave us, or the chicken or bean plant, etc. I would say it lightly, but mean it from my heart.*

Kristin N. contributed her family tradition: *My husband and I use family meetings to teach gratitude. Every week our family sits down for our meeting and the first thing we do is go around and say something nice about each member of the family. And each 'thing' has to start out with 'I appreciate...' Not only does this help us to look at the positives and be grateful for our family members but also teaches us how to accept gratitude from other people.*

Other Gratitude Traditions

Besides prayers, there are other ways of creating traditions of gratitude that might work for you family:

Family Gratitude Journal - create a ritual and a keepsake at the same time. During dinner (picking a special night can help), at your family meetings, or during holidays and birthdays - have someone write down each member's gratitudes. This can also be done on the family calendar if there's room. For older children, you can encourage them to keep their own journals.

Gratitude Jar Version 1: Having a jar displayed prominently in your home that you contribute a quarter to - every time you have something good happen for you. When the jar is full - give it to a charity or someone you know who is in need.

Gratitude Jar Version 2: Periodically write small notes of gratitude and drop them in the jar. At special family times (dinner, meetings, holidays) or for a quick reminder, pull some notes out and share them.

Birthday Gratitude Jar: Leading up to a birthday, other members of the house fill a jar with their gratitudes for the person of honor.

I know of a man who sends a bouquet of flowers to his mom every year on HIS birthday - thanking her for having him!

Birthday/Anniversary Traditions:
Have the birthday celebrant say or write a list:

- 5 Things I'm Grateful for at 5
- 10 Things I'm Grateful for at 10
- Couples Bonus: 20 Things I'm Grateful For About You - on our 20th anniversary

3 Good Things: It's as simple as it sounds. Every night at bed time, or at a special family time, have everyone recount 3 good things from their day. This exercise has been tested scientifically and found to produce more optimism and positivity. As long as it's not imposed or used to rush through a disappointment this can be a great way to refocus.

Gratitude Activities & Games

The Glad Game - Read the book Pollyanna or watch the Disney version then play the game. How can you find something to be glad about in the situations that come up in your day?

Count Your Blessings - At dinner or in the car, go in a round and see how many blessings you can list. Nice way to model your own appreciation and to hear where your kids are at.

Gratigories: A downloadable card game for purchase at http://www.lasarafirefox.com/products.html Basic set has 40 different categories to consider something you are grateful for. Great for a long car ride with kids.

Gratitude Turkey: Craft projects are another avenue for teaching children about gratitude. This activity was found on: www.christian-mommies.com Designing a gratitude turkey made out of construction paper. Each day in November, take a colorful paper feather and write something on it for which each child is grateful. It is a fun way to remind them of the things they have.

Volunteering & Community Service

Most English teachers will tell you that one of the best principles in writing is the Show, Don't Tell principle. The idea is that showing a character's personality rather than telling about the character is more powerful. Gratitude is the same way.

Telling someone or yourself that you are grateful is good, but showing your appreciation is even better. Volunteering and community service do that.

T.S. of Minneapolis posted this on a blog: *Instead of talking only about what blessings we are thankful for, we think about what we can GIVE to make others be thankful. For example, my 5-year old said he is thankful for nature so we gave to nature by cleaning up a park.*

In keeping with this idea, if your children are grateful for your great family, why not invite someone who doesn't have this kind of love to your holiday celebration or just to dinner some time. That is a way to show your gratitude for the love you receive.

Family Giving Day - Birthdays are for getting: getting gifts, getting cards, getting special attention, getting your favorite dinner and a cake. But it can be nice to spend some time giving as well. A Family Giving Day may include: giving to others, donating your time, or sacrificing an expensive dinner and giving the money to a worthy cause.

Volunteering
Here are some suggestions for ways to get your children involved in giving:

• Help out a relative or a neighbor with yard work, not for money but out of kindness as a way to give gratitude.

(Not that kids can't have a shoveling or babysitting service - just consider that sometimes they offer to help people for free.)

- Bake cookies or meals for people who are shut-in

- Fill a grocery bag at the store with food for the local women's center

- Volunteer at a homeless shelter or the humane society

- Get your children involved in adopting a family for Christmas or buying and donating toys to Toys-For-Tots

Sturdy and Kathy McK. and their family participated in the program through their local fire station: *We explained to them what we were doing beforehand and then took them to the store to pick out a toy to give to another child. They each ended up picking out 2 and we then took those to the fire station to donate them. The firefighters were impressed that the kids brought the toys, and gave us a full tour of the firehouse, trucks, pole, and equipment they use for rescues and breathing in the fires. The kids got to do something nice and have a great time, too.*

- Assist your child in going through their toys and clothes and donating them to charity - while talking about the reasons you are doing this

- Have a lemonade stand or even a backyard carnival to raise money for a good cause

- Visit a nursing home on a monthly basis and play cards or games with some of the residents (though be gentle with young children because it can be a bit intimidating to them.)

Sue C. considers service so important that she has occasionally taken her children out of school to volunteer for a service project. *It's a different kind of learning and one that can be extremely valuable.*

Of course teaching your child to be a respectful volunteer is crucial as well. Being careful to convey a caring, rather than a pitying, attitude is important.

Out of all the ways to nurture and inspire gratitude in children, volunteering can be the most powerful. Giving children an opportunity to appreciate what they have by being exposed to, and giving back to, the world beyond their home can allow them to come away with a new appreciation for the part of the world that is their home.

Conclusion

Gratitude is not a one time discussion or deed. Cultivating and growing gratitude is a long term endeavor. Planting, watering, tilling the soil, adding fertilizer, weeding, pruning, appreciating and helping your child enjoy their harvest takes time, patience, and care.

Don't overwhelm yourself with stress or worry that you are not doing enough. Or that your kids are never going to get it. Just find ways to practice something. Commit to one suggestion in this book that resonated with you and your family. And then on another day, try something else.

Bringing children up to notice and appreciate the world that sustains and nurtures them is a noble parenting goal. Done well, there is a very good chance that they really will thank you for it later.

As I tell my children, "It's my job is to keep you safe, clothe you, feed you, teach you, give you love. My job is not to make you happy. That is your job. But I can teach you this: The path to happiness is gratitude.

Thanks for reading, good luck and take care...

Thanksgiving Day

Sometimes thanksgiving messages get lost behind the catching up, gravy, football scores and store circulars for the next day's shopping mission. But making sure that the discussion and practice of gratitude have a prominent seat at the table is important. Besides the ideas from the last chapter, here are some other ways to include it on this day:

- Go around the table sharing special prayers and thankful sentiments to help everyone remember the reason for the gathering. This can be done informally or with more flair. For those who don't like to speak up in a crowd, prior to the meal you can designate someone to bring around slips of paper and a pen and have people submit a gratitude. At the dinner table, one person can read them (maybe having others guess who wrote them - to make it more fun.)

- If some family are missing from the day, have them send a gratitude beforehand or use the phone or computer to be 'present' at your gratitude moment.

- If your family has lost someone important, depending on where people are in the grieving process, having those gathered share what they think that person would have said is a way of bringing your loved one's spirit into the day.

- If you want to go to the next level, as discussed in Chapter 8, doing gratitude can be incorporated into the day through community service.

Appendix
Saying Thank You

Feeling gratitude and not expressing it is like wrapping a present and not giving it. ~ **William Arthur Ward**

Where Are You?

Parent skill for teaching children to say 'thank you' runs the gambit. Some parents are as oblivious as their children to the gifts their children receive. Some parents are just too overwhelmed to find time to teach their children these lessons. Some parents do it for their children. And on the other end of the spectrum are parents that just don't let up. These parents have taken the importance of saying 'thank you' beyond reasonable expectations and will reprimand or shame their child for every infraction.

Most parents, luckily, are somewhere in the middle and are aware of their role in teaching this skill to their children, and try to incorporate it into their expectations.

Those parents that are part-time politeness police might be on to something as long as there is enough time on the clock. And there is both modeling and discussion about the importance of saying 'thank you' that needs to be done on a regular basis.

Here are some specific ideas for saying or writing gratitudes.

Verbal And Written Thank Yous

Sometimes, a verbal 'thank you' or a call is fine. But sometimes things need to be written down for posterity. Putting a 'thank you' on paper, offers you the opportunity to relive the kind deed again. Writing a thank you can give you double the gratitude.

As your children grow, the amount of effort they put into thank yous should grow with them. Here are some steps along the way:

Babies: Babies have it made. You do all the work and they just lay there and enjoy it. And writing 'thank you' is no exception. They get the gift but YOU have to do the thanking. How fair is that? Oh well - I guess we get to have a little more gratitude practice ourselves. Here's an idea: Take a picture of your baby with the gift and send it with the thank you.

Saying Thank You

Toddlers

- You write the card and read it to your child
- Talk about the giver in positive ways
- Have them scribble their name or draw a picture, put on the stamp, put the letter in the mailbox

3-5 Year Olds

- Play Secretary
- Have them make the card and sign it
- Dictate to you what they want to say (With/without sentence starters from you)

6-10 Year Olds

- Have them draw, computer generate, or pick a card, working with them on what to say, and helping them address the envelope

11 & Up

- They should be choosing, or generating a card, writing, addressing, stamping and mailing it themselves

Helpful rules: Write card before you get to use gift

As trust and habit are established - step down

Hold them to it with consequences

E-Thank Yous

Sending a thank you via e-mail or text messaging is controversial - especially with older, less techno-savvy folks. But children are growing up with different ways of communicating than we did so some openness to doing things differently seems reasonable.

Talking with your child about whether the receiver of the card would appreciate this new form of gratitude might help. If the gift giver is happenin' it might be fine but if you know they would prefer a written card, then going the extra mile is a nice gesture.

The point that the gift giver probably thought of your child when they picked the gift - so thinking of the giver when sending a thank you - might register some logic and assist in your case for the written card. Plus the thought that learning how to write a note, address an envelope, and go the extra step to say, "I REALLY appreciated your gift," has lots of benefits.

On the other hand, don't be an old fogey. Moving forward with the times requires some flexibility on our parts as well.

What to Say & Write - Being Specific

There is an art to saying 'thank you' that can actually feel better for both the receiver AND the giver! When you add specific details, when you recall an event or moment, this makes the gratitude more powerful.

I once accompanied my youngest son on a 3 day school camping trip. Before leaving on the last day, the students invited the camp counselors and cooks to the common room to thank them for their efforts. We asked the students to thank them in very specific ways. As the children went around in the circle, you could see them thinking. Some said, the spaghetti. Several recalled the scary camp story , dramatically told by one of the counselors at the campfire. One recalled the Predator-Prey game.

About half way through the exchange - one of the cooks ran into the kitchen to get a helper who had not come out. She wanted her to hear this outpouring of gratitude. That's how good it felt.

Eileen C. shared the a great story about how valued a card can be: *I made sure that my son, Tim, always sent thank you notes for presents and for anything special that someone did for him. My brothers each took Tim on vacation with them at different times in his life.*

Recently we were at a family gathering and my brother pulled out a thank you letter that my son had sent to his uncle for taking him on a fishing trip years ago. It was so sweet to see what Tim had written - thanking his uncle and then going on to say he was so glad that his uncle had caught the biggest fish and won the pool. I tried to get the letter so that I could put it in an album but my brother wouldn't part with it :-)

Prompts for more powerful gratitudes:

I am grateful for...because...
Thank you for...It really came in handy when I...
I so appreciate that you...it really helped with...

The Gratitude Letter

This exercise came from an experiment in positive psychology. Trying to discover what increases life satisfaction, a group of participants were asked to think of a person who has supported them and write them a letter detailing their gratitude. Sending it was optional but participants reported great experiences not only from writing the letters but also if they did have an opportunity to share it with the person they had identified.

This activity can be done with adolescents as a way to counter some of that natural self-centeredness that descends upon them in their teen years. And parents can do it for themselves!

Appendix
How To Be A Good Giver

The desire to be appreciated for our thoughtfulness, noticed for our contributions, and valued for our deeds is somewhat universal. The trouble comes when our need for appreciation trumps the gesture, the deed isn't that thoughtful or respectful, or has strings attached.

How freely are you giving the gift? Is it just something on your checklist of 'have to's? Is the gift secretly a bribe for influencing the recipient? What is the spirit of your giving? Is it a gift for because you care or are you feel you have to help the receiver of your 'generosity' because they are a mess. (If you gave this book as a gift - please tell me you didn't hand it to a parent with a - here, you REALLY need this. But rather - I thought of you when I saw this because you're always trying hard to be a good mom (dad). And this looked like something that could help.)

Some giving is not very thoughtfully done. I remember talking with a volunteer medical missionary who went to impoverished countries. She shared the phrase, 'Junk for Jesus'. It referred to some of the donations that made their way there - but that weren't of any quality, or were not appropriate for the climate or conditions of the recipients. The apparent mindset of the giver was that it was better than nothing - but honestly not by much. Expecting gratitude in these instances is unreasonable. If you are giving to another person - it is the responsibility of the giver to try to be thoughtful.

This applies to giving help as well. When you see a person struggling - perhaps a child tying his shoes, a friend sharing a relationship dilemma, or person with a disability - do you jump in without asking?

Taking over, offering unasked for advice, or insisting on helping isn't very helpful. Applying a good helper philosophy to dealing with your children is also essential. How about with a child who can't do their math homework? Jumping in to help isn't necessarily the best thing - and will often be met with ingratitude. Try being empathetic: "It looks like a hard one." Try being confident: "I think you can get this." Try being respectful: "Do you want my help?"

GRATITUDE RESOURCES

Reading stories and news articles or watching shows and talking about how lucky you are can have a big impact on gratitude. (Note: Consider the age and temperament of your child when determining appropriate stories and when exposing your children to life's more serious realities.)

BOOKS For CHILDREN:

Berenstein Bears Get the Gimmes by Stan & Jan Berenstein A great story to help your kids see this concept in action

Pollyanna (book and movie are different) An interesting journey into taking gratitude to the extreme.

Turn Of The Century: Eleven Centuries of Children and Change by Ellen Jackson An opportunity to gain perspective, by learning about what children of different eras were doing.

The Presents' Presents by Teresa de Grosbois. A story about giving instead of getting birthday presents as a way of teaching gratitude. e-book: www.smallshifts.com

From the Bible: *Jesus cures the lepers* - *Luke 17:11-19* Jesus cures 10 lepers and only 1 comes back to say thank you. Puts it in perspective - I mean cured of leprosy and only 1 thought to say thank you?

The Hundred Dresses by Eleanor Estes A story about charity and people who may have less than we do.

The Diary of Ann Frank by Ann Frank - Story of the concealment of a Jewish family during WW2.

What To Do When Good Enough Isn't Good Enough The Real Deal on Perfectionism: A Guide for Kids - Thomas S. Greenspon, Ph.D. www.freespirit.com

BOOKS For GROWN-UPS

Thanks! How The New Science of Gratitude Can Make You Happier! by Robert A. Emmons

The How of Happiness: A New Approach to Getting the Life You Want by Sonja Lyubomirsky

The Happiness Project: Etc by Gretchen Rubin A personal journey to find out what makes you happy based on science

GRATITUDE QUOTES TO PONDER

The only people with whom you should try to get even are those who have helped you. ~ **John E. Southard**

If a fellow isn't thankful for what he's got, he isn't likely to be thankful for what he's going to get. ~ **Frank A. Clark**

Gratitude is a quality similar to electricity: it must be produced and discharged and used up in order to exist at all. ~ **William Faulkner**

I feel a very unusual sensation - if it is not indigestion, I think it must be gratitude. ~ **Benjamin Disraeli**

There is no greater difference between men than between grateful and ungrateful people. ~ **R.H. Blyth**

As we express our gratitude, we must never forget that the highest appreciation is not to utter words, but to live by them. ~ **John F. Kennedy**

At times our own light goes out and is rekindled by a spark from another person. Each of us has cause to think with deep gratitude of those who have lighted the flame within us. ~ **Albert Schweitzer**

Gratitude is a vaccine, an antitoxin, and an antiseptic. ~ **John Henry Jowett**

Appreciation can make a day, even change a life. Your willingness to put it into words is all that is necessary. ~ **Margaret Cousins**